Editor-in-Chief and Founder:
  Lyndon H. LaRouche, Jr.
Editorial Board: *Lyndon H. LaRouche, Jr. , Helga
  Zepp-LaRouche, Robert Ingraham, Tony
  Papert, Gerald Rose, Dennis Small, Jeffrey
  Steinberg, William Wertz*
Co-Editors: *Robert Ingraham, Tony Papert*
Technology: *Marsha Freeman*
Transcriptions: *Katherine Notley*
Ebooks: *Richard Burden*
Graphics: *Alan Yue*
Photos: *Stuart Lewis*
Circulation Manager: *Stanley Ezrol*

INTELLIGENCE DIRECTORS
Economics: *Marcia Merry Baker, Paul Gallagher*
History: *Anton Chaitkin*
Ibero-America: *Dennis Small*
Russia and Eastern Europe: *Rachel Douglas*
United States: *Debra Freeman*

INTERNATIONAL BUREAUS
Bogotá: *Miriam Redondo*
Berlin: *Rainer Apel*
Copenhagen: *Tom Gillesberg*
Lima: *Sara Madueño*
Melbourne: *Robert Barwick*
Mexico City: *Gerardo Castilleja Chávez*
New Delhi: *Ramtanu Maitra*
Paris: *Christine Bierre*
Stockholm: *Ulf Sandmark*
United Nations, N.Y.C.: *Leni Rubinstein*
Washington, D.C.: *William Jones*
Wiesbaden: *Göran Haglund*

ON THE WEB
e-mail: eirns@larouchepub.com
www.larouchepub.com
www.executiveintelligencereview.com
www.larouchepub.com/eiw
Webmaster: *John Sigerson*
Assistant Webmaster: *George Hollis*
Editor, Arabic-language edition: *Hussein Askary*

EIR (ISSN 0273-6314) *is published weekly
(50 issues), by EIR News Service, Inc.,
P.O. Box 17390, Washington, D.C. 20041-0390.
(703) 297-8434*

European Headquarters: E.I.R. GmbH, Postfach
Bahnstrasse 9a, D-65205, Wiesbaden, Germany
Tel: 49-611-73650
Homepage: http://www.eir.de
e-mail: info@eir.de
Director: Georg Neudecker

Montreal, Canada: 514-461-1557
eir@eircanada.ca

Denmark: EIR - Danmark, Sankt Knuds Vej 11,
basement left, DK-1903 Frederiksberg, Denmark.
Tel.: +45 35 43 60 40, Fax: +45 35 43 87 57. e-mail:
cirdk@hotmail.com.

Mexico City: EIR, Sor Juana Inés de la Cruz 242-2
Col. Agricultura C.P. 11360
Delegación M. Hidalgo, México D.F.
Tel. (5525) 5318-2301
eirmexico@gmail.com

The Mass Strike and the 2018 Election

This Election Will Not Be 2016 Done Over— We're Way Beyond That Now!

by Tony Papert

Oct. 7—Those like Hillary Clinton who have never understood what happened in the 2016 election, naturally expect (and hope) that the 2018 midterms will mark a return to "normal" U.S. elections. They make nonsense predictions, like their claim that a statistic—the one that says that on average, Presidents have usually lost in midterm elections—ensures Trump will lose the House of Representatives. But nothing could be more ludicrous than to believe that any statistic from the past could control what Americans do now. It could only influence them if they were stupid enough to believe such an argument. But now, in fact, Americans generally are a lot less stupid than they were two years ago—or even two months ago. That is the real story of this election— although it is one that Hillary Clinton may never be able to understand.

The name for this phenomenon is "the mass strike," as Lyndon LaRouche constructed this argument exactly 50 years ago, basing himself on Percy Bysshe Shelley's unfinished *A Defence of Poetry* of 1821, and Rosa Luxemburg's *The Mass Strike, the Political Party and the Trade Unions* of 1906. Great works by two of humanity's greatest leaders of the modern era. LaRouche most frequently cited a section towards the end of Shelley's work, assuming his hearers were familiar with the writing as a whole. Describing historical periods preceding or accompanying "a great and free development of the national will" of England, Shelley wrote, "At such periods there is an accumulation of the power of communicating and receiving intense and impassioned conceptions respecting man and nature."

The spread of this "power" is not precisely voluntary, and is often unnoticed by the recipients. Its immediate causes in one or another case are usually unknown—as is seen both in Shelley's and in Luxemburg's arguments. Indeed it most resembles a perception rather than a thought—but not a perception by the usual organs of sense. Shelley continues from the sentence quoted above, to write "The persons in whom this power resides, may often, as far as regards many portions of their nature, have little apparent correspondence with that spirit of good of which they are the ministers. But even whilst they deny and abjure, they are yet compelled to serve, the power which is seated on the throne of their own soul."

If we can prevent the disaster of a Democratic House of Representatives, which would destroy the country by impeaching the President; if we can shut down Britain's regime-change operation and put conspirators Obama, Mueller, Brennan and others in jail; and if we can use this mass-strike period to win hegemony for LaRouche's "Four New Laws" and New Bretton Woods system—then, under those conditions, the whole world is now entering a new period of deep-going, far-reaching positive reform, comparable to Franklin Roosevelt's New Deal, but far broader in its implications. National sovereignty is being brought back from the dead, at the same time that sovereign nations fully engage together to win the "common aims of mankind," as LaRouche's collaborator the late Dr. Edward Teller put it.

What is all this—a forecast of the future? ("Never make predictions, especially about the future," said Casey Stengel.) But its effects are already here today, in what Shelley called "the gigantic shadows which futurity casts upon the present." You can call it the future if you like, but it is already shaping the 2018 elections, as it has been for some time before we noticed it. The "power" Shelley was writing about, we might call intensely awakened individual creativity—which is intrinsically social at the same time that it is individual. It is the only conscious power of negative entropy we know of in the universe. Its effects are seen in the volunteers joining Kesha Rogers' flagship Independent campaign in Texas' 9th Congressional District, but also equally in thousands of other ways which may seem to have nothing to do with each other.

How does it work? Americans (and not only Americans) are experiencing the most diverse kinds of effects, minute-to-minute, of all the indirect ramifications of the fact that the long nightmare which reached the deepest level of Hell under George W. Bush and Obama, may finally be coming to an end. (There are many other valid ways to phrase this as well.) This reflects itself, unawares, in changed personal relationships, in cultural factors, and other areas too numerous to name. People, even if unaware of it, at the same time are changed by a perception, as it were, of something "gigantic" of which they are unaware.

A sort of reasoning is going on in their minds which is often implicit, rather than conscious. (Rosa Luxemburg's *Mass Strike* explores this aspect very fully.) Take, as an example, the effects of the Kavanaugh hearings. What is their meaning for tens of millions of Americans, even if they themselves may not be aware of that meaning? "Think where we'd be now had Hillary won in 2016. What an open sewer!" And where we will be if she claws her way back.

The major "Russiagate" documents which are being declassified by President Trump and Congressional committees will, over the next few days, intersect this mass-strike process.

The mass strike is occurring in the forcing-medium of the oncoming election. What does it mean for the "election per se"? Not only will this not be a "normal" pre-2016 election geometry. It will not be a rerun of 2016 either—we're now in a completely different world from where we were in 2016. Among many other effects, the mass strike means that unique creative interventions will be made, by ourselves and others, and ourselves with others, to "turn the adversary's flank," and such interventions will re-echo and inspire all sorts of others, increasingly as Nov. 6 approaches.

EIR Contents

www.larouchepub.com Volume 45, Number 41, October 12, 2018

Portrait by Alfred Clint (1929)   Unknown photographer (c.1895-1905)

Italy Confronts EU, Works with Trump and China

by Claudio Celani

Oct. 7—A hundred days after its inauguration, the Italian "populist" government has kicked over the chessboard in Europe and internationally in an unprecedented way, playing a major role in the ongoing paradigm change in global politics and foreshadowing an early demise for the corrupt elites that have ruled over Europe in the last decades.

Italy is opening the Mediterranean to the Chinese Belt and Road Initiative, disrupting the EU sabotage of the BRI, while building an alliance with Trump's USA and Putin's Russia to stabilize North Africa by favoring the super-power dialogue and pushing for economic development. At the same time, Rome is resolutely challenging EU's austerity policy under the motto "Italians first, the EU after."

The two coalition partners, the Lega and the Five Star Movement (M5S) are very different in many ways, and at times almost antagonistic, but they have managed to agree on a government program that emphasizes common positive features of both election platforms aimed at asserting national interests. The most important such feature is the new approach towards China and the Belt and Road policy.

Task Force China & African Development

Under the initiative of Under Secretary of State Michele Geraci, the Italian government has set up a Task Force China with the aim of "guaranteeing Italy a position of leadership in Europe vis-à-vis China's Belt and Road and Made in China 2025 initiatives," as the ministry for Economic Development (MISE) announced

UNDP/Lamine Bal

Italy leads new way for Europe: Under Secretary of State Michele Geraci (left) builds Italy's partnership in China's Belt and Road Initiative; African development focus on the Italian Transaqua project to revitalize Lake Chad (shown above) Lake Chad Conference, Berlin, Sept. 3, 2018; in favor of super-power dialogue, Prime Minister Giuseppe Conte meets with President Trump (below), July 30, 2018.

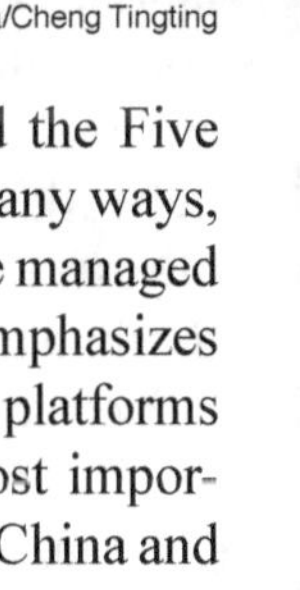

Xinhua/Cheng Tingting

White House/Stephanie Chasez

in a release Aug. 20 (see box, page 7). The Task Force held its first meeting Oct. 1 with about 300 participants, including government members, journalists, businessmen, academicians and others. The meeting was addressed by Geraci and the Chinese ambassador to Italy, Li Ruiyu.

Geraci has visited China twice in that interval, the second time with Luigi Di Maio, Italy's Deputy Prime

Minister and Minister for Economic Development. They signed a Memorandum of Understanding (MoU) to promote economic cooperation with China's Sichuan province and start negotiations for a strategic partnership in Belt and Road projects, especially in Africa. A MoU on such a strategic partnership is expected to be signed by the two countries before the end of the year. Minister Di Maio declared Sept. 20: "We are very happy to be the only G-7 country that has carried on such advanced negotiations on the Belt and Road Initiative."

Artist conception of the proposed Strait of Messina Bridge, to connect the Island of Sicily and the Italian peninsula. When built, it will be the world's longest single-span suspension bridge.

As the charter of Task Force China explains, the primary focus of cooperation with China sought by Italy is Africa. The Italian government is convinced that China's approach in Africa is the right one and that European nations should help China to develop Africa—and thus solve the migration problem at its root, and to be a driver for self-development.

It has been recognized that the key to China's success in Africa is the focus on infrastructure development. There are also good reasons to believe that the new Italian government will give a new boost to the Italian Transaqua project to revitalize Lake Chad, which will involve large water-transfers, new electricity generation, improved transportation and increased agricultural production. Transaqua was approved at the International Lake Chad Conference last February in Abuja, Nigeria and the previous Italian government had endorsed it, issuing a grant to co-finance the feasibility study. Joint Italian-Chinese cooperation on Transaqua has already been established between the Italian Bonifica firm (the authors of the project) and China's PowerChina.

Geraci endorsed Transaqua as a model of tripartite Africa-China-Europe cooperation when he was a professor of Economics in Shanghai. The future undersecretary of the Economic Development ministry published an article by this author in his blog, calling it "an example to be studied by our policy makers".

Italy & China to Develop Southern Italy

Italy is seeking Chinese cooperation not only to develop Africa, but also to upgrade its own infrastructure within the framework of the BRI. Under the previous government, Rome had joined the Maritime Silk Road, offering to upgrade the ports of Genoa and Trieste, on the Tyrrhenian and Adriatic Seas. However, even bigger plans are possible, focussing on developing infrastructure throughout Southern Italy. Indeed, China had already shown interest in such ideas in 2011, proposing to: upgrade the deep-sea ports in Sicily and Calabria; help build the bridge over the Messina Strait connecting Sicily to the mainland; and upgrade road and rail connections to link up with Italy's high-speed network, which currently stops at Salerno. Additionally, an international airport to be built in the center of Sicily would function as a hub for connections to both Africa and North-Central Europe.

Those plans were aborted by interventions of Hillary Clinton, then U.S. Secretary of State, who represented U.S. opposition to that cooperation, and by the EU, which toppled the Italian government and replaced it with its puppet Mario Monti, who cancelled all investments.

Such an ambitious project could now be resumed. Both Geraci, a Sicilian, and Prime Minister Giuseppe Conte, have indicated that the government will have a new focus on the development of Southern Italy.

One of the obstacles in 2011, Hillary Clinton, has

been removed. The other obstacle, the EU, is still there and has already opened a three-front war against Italy.

As Bloomberg recognized Oct. 4,

With its pivot to China, Italy's populist coalition risks alienating European Union allies just as it has on migration, fiscal policy and its scorn for the EU itself. Italy's last government, under Prime Minister Paolo Gentiloni, had joined Germany and France at the forefront of EU-wide efforts to curb Chinese investment in critical infrastructure and strategic companies.

The new government in Rome has ditched that drive, according to Geraci, who said he didn't want a common EU policy on screening outside investments. "We have 28 different economies with 28 different interests," he said. Rather, Italy will push to do business with China "within the scope of our existing alliances with the EU, with NATO," he said.

Giovanni Tria, Minister of Economy and Finance.

Geraci dismissed any concerns that Italy could get in too deep with China and face a debt risk. Sri Lanka, for instance, borrowed from China to build a port and then couldn't repay the loans. Italy could learn about "what pitfalls we may be running into" from Sri Lanka, Malaysia and Laos, he said, but Italy has other issues.

"Our European friends already have a lot of Italian debt, we don't need to worry about China, it's the European Central Bank that has Italian debt," Geraci said. "The size of the Italian economy saves us from this debt trap."

Geraci speaks fluent Chinese, and he is not alone in the cabinet: Economy (Finance) Minister Tria speaks Chinese too, as he was involved for many years with China when he was Professor at the University of Rome Tor Vergata, before he was appointed to the cabinet. Indeed, Tria's first trip abroad as a minister was not to

Italy Leads the Way for Belt & Road in Europe

Italy wants to take the leadership for the Belt and Road Initiative in Europe. The Italian Task Force China set up last August, includes in its aims:

"Helping Italian companies participate in Chinese investment programs, financed by the Belt and Road Initiative both in China and along the entire route of the New Silk Road, at the same time stimulating investments in and transfer of Chinese know-how to develop infrastructure, energy and transport networks in Italy. With 25,000 km of high-speed trains already built and 21,000 km more planned, to just mention one of the many possible examples, China is currently the country that more than any

other in the world has the best knowledge in the sector of infrastructural development."

Another point in the Task Force charter says:

"China can help Italy solve the immigration problem by helping Africa: China is the country that has invested the most in Africa (already $340 billion, much more than the $70 billion usually estimated by analysts), with effects that are already visible in terms of the impact on poverty rates and which, in the long term, should gradually help reduce migration flows towards Europe. China's involvement in Africa offers Italy a historic opportunity of international cooperation for the socio-economic stabilization of the continent, crucial not only for a sustainable and socially responsible solution of the immigration problem, but also for the economic opportunities that will arise in the continent for Italian firms."

Brussels, as in the EU tradition, but to Beijing at the end of August.

Against EU 'Stability & (No) Growth Pact'

The other two fronts opened against the EU are migration policy and fiscal policy.

On migration, Italy has put an end to the failed EU policy of forcing the country to rescue at sea and receive thousands of illegal immigrants who want to reach northern Europe, but

Ministry of the Interior

Matteo Salvini, Minister of the Interior.

forcing them to stay in Italy, and at the same time enforcing economic recipes that make such a policy unsustainable.

Matteo Salvini, Italy's Interior Minister and Deputy PM, successfully chased away NGO ships that were suspected of colluding with human traffickers in North Africa, and in some cases refused to allow them to enter Italian ports. Salvini's resolute attitude has provoked scornful and hypocritical reactions from several EU Commissioners and French President Emmanuel Macron, who is well known for rejecting thousands of immigrants at the French-Italian border.

On fiscal policy, the new Italian government has created a budget that includes a strong social component, as well as investment for growth. The EU-enforced austerity had thrown the Italian economy into a serious recession especially since 2011, pushing more than seven million people

Paolo Savona, Minister of European Affairs.

into poverty and slashing production to one third below the levels of 2008.

The EU "Stability and Growth Pact" mandates that so-called indebted countries reduce their budget deficit to zero by slashing their budgets every year. Italy had followed that rule. The previous government, before leaving last May, drafted a budget plan based on a 0.8% deficit in the GDP rate.

The Conte government scrapped that plan and presented a budget draft based on a 2.4% deficit for the next three years, eventually changing it to 2.4% in 2019 and decreasing the deficit the following two years. This would make about 45 billion Euro available for (a) an increase of minimum pensions to 780 Euro, (b) a general unemployment check of the same amount, (c) a flat tax for small and medium enterprises (SME), (d) a tax cut for SMEs that reinvest in equipment and employment, (e) a fund to reimburse victims of bank bail-in procedures, and (f) 15 billion Euro more in investment above the previously planned 36 billion Euro.

In presenting the budget to the EU Commission, Paolo Savona, Italy's Minister for EU Affairs (and the most prestigious member of the government), said that Italy had "thrown down the gauntlet to the Old Europe. Now we must win the war, because it will be war."

Indeed, the EU reaction was just short of sending bombers to Rome. On Oct. 1, EU Commission President Jean-Claude Juncker declared in a press conference that "Italy is distancing itself from the budgetary targets we have jointly agreed at EU level. If Italy wants further special treatment, that would mean the end of the Euro. So, you have to be very strict." And on Oct. 5, EU Commissioners Valdis Dombrovskis and Pierre Moscovici sent a letter to Italian Economy Minister Giovanni Tria, claiming that Italy's deficit targets were a "source of serious concern." The move is out of protocol and resembles, albeit at a lower level, the "ultimatum" sent in summer 2011 to the Italian government by Mario Draghi and Jean-Claude Trichet, respectively incoming and outgoing chairman of the European Central Bank, which started the economic warfare and the coup that eventually replaced Italy's legitimate government with an EU-executioner cabinet led by Mario Monti.

The content of the letter was leaked to the Italian daily *La Repubblica*: "We call on the Italian authorities to ensure that the [budget] will be in compliance with the common fiscal rules and look forward to seeing the details of the measures," said the two-page letter, of which *La Repubblica* published excerpts.

That same day, it was revealed that ECB chairman Mario Draghi had flown to Rome Oct. 3 to secretly meet Italian State President Sergio Mattarella. Media accounts of the meeting indicate that Draghi outlined the threat of a financial assault on Italy if the government goes too far with the budget. Draghi, Brussels, Paris and Berlin are very well aware of the fact that the winds of change coming from Italy will fill the sails of "populists" throughout Europe, who will sweep the elections for European Parliament next spring. This would mean the end of austerity policies and, in perspective, the Euro.

For this reason, they are engaged in a desperate attempt to crush the Italian government in the cradle, so to speak. In doing this, they are willing to start a financial crisis which could get out of control. A repetition of the 2011 scenario, when the EU toppled the Berlusconi-Tremonti government, would mean a downgrading of the Italian sovereign debt and a dramatic increase of refinancing costs for the Italian government on international markets. This, in turn, would provoke a crisis for all those banks that own such assets—basically, the entire national banking system. In 2011 these tactics worked, and under international and media pressure, the Berlusconi government resigned.

Under Attack, Government Popularity Rises

This time it will be different. Sen. Alberto Bagnai, a leading economist and current chairman of the Senate Banking Committee, made it clear in a speech he gave in Ascoli Piceno on Sept. 29 that the government and Parliament will not back down to EU schemes. Bagnai announced that in the coming weeks, his committee will focus on two things: an investigating commission on banks and the so-called EU Banking Union.

Bagnai blasted the "one piece of the Banking Union" dealing with non-performing loans (NPLs). Behind the nice words used there, Bagnai said, "what they want is your homes! They demand to have them without going through the courts and they want them quick."

That is the reality behind the so-called "secondary market for NPLs" that the ECB wants to set up, forcing banks to sell NPLs for ten cents on the dollar to vulture funds, which will then expropriate the assets attached to the loans.

Senator Alberto Bagnai

"The bail-in should be called by its real name: Expropriation," Bagnai stated, making it clear that in a financial crash the Italian government won't expropriate bank customers. The government has already set up a 15 billion Euro fund to reimburse small bondholders hit by the "resolution" of local banks in Veneto and in central Italy in 2017.

In an indirect answer to the Dombrovskis-Moscovici letter, Bagnai tweeted: "They are ridiculous. Imposing austerity has created enough problems for us, as also where they come from. Those Fathers of Europe, who believe that their daughter will run faster by offloading one of her manufacturing legs, are dangerous but above all ridiculous."

That austerity kills was dramatically demonstrated Aug. 14 with the collapse of the Morandi highway bridge in Genoa, which killed 43 and paralyzed a strategic road connection on the North-South Rotterdam-Genoa trade route. As revealed in a government investigation, the private concession running the road (and the bridge) had omitted necessary maintenance and failed to act on a serious warning before the collapse. Autostrade per l'Italia, owned by the Benetton family (of clothing fame), had spent an average of only 23,000 Euro per year! Furthermore, the company had lied to government inspectors, reporting stability checks which never occurred.

The Genoa tragedy has fueled popular anger against

the EU, as privatizations and austerity are two faces of the same coin: neo-liberal policies imposed with Italy's early entrance into the Euro.

In this context, the more the EU and the establishment media attack the government, the more the government popularity grows. According to the monthly Ipsos poll released at the beginning of October, the Lega runs at 34% (doubling the March 4, 2018 election result!), followed by the M5S at 28.5%. The government has a 64% approval rating, gaining not only among Lega and M5S voters (94 and 92) but also among opposition forces. PM Conte has an even higher rating (67), followed by Salvini (57) and Di Maio (52).

Conti-Trump 'Preferential Relationship'

A significant factor in the equation is the "preferential relationship" between Conte and Trump, established with Conte's visit to the White House last July 30 (see https://larouchepub.com/other/2018/4532-trump_conte.html), and consolidated at the United Nations General Assembly, where the two leaders had lunch together Sept. 26.

This alliance achieved its first success at the UN Security Council, when the French proposal to held elections in Libya next December was voted down thanks to the United States, which is backing the Italian position that conditions must first be created for such a vote to be successful, i.e., an agreement among all major factions. The next step would be an international conference on Libya to be held in Palermo, Sicily, Nov. 11-12, where either Trump or Secretary of State Pompeo should participate.

Italy is also playing a mediating role between the USA and Iran.

According to a U.S. diplomatic source who spoke to the Italian daily *La Verità*, "Washington cannot completely drop Iran for security reasons, and in the current scenario, Italy represents the perfect bridge, because only Italy, among major European countries, showed willingness to work with Trump's United States."

At the UN, after his discussion with Trump, Italian Prime Minister Giuseppe Conte met with Iranian President Hassan Rouhani, and Conte's diplomatic advisor Pietro Benassi had a long talk with National Security Advisor John Bolton, which focused on Libya, but also included Iran.

NEW RELEASE, **Volume II**

The New Silk Road Becomes the World Land-Bridge:

A Shared Future For Humanity

The spirit of the New Silk Road is changing the world for the better. The exciting overview in this new 440-page Volume II report updates the roadmap given in Volume I, on the coming into being of the World Land-Bridge for development and peace. BRICS countries have a strategy to prevent war and economic catastrophe. It's time for the rest of the world to join!

Includes:

Introduction by Helga Zepp-LaRouche, "A Shared Future for Humanity."

Progress Reports on development corridors worldwide, spurred by China's Belt and Road Initiative. Features 140 maps.

Principles of Physical Economy by Lyndon LaRouche, especially his "Four Laws" for emergency action in the Trans-Atlantic.

Soft cover (440 pages)
Domestic Price: $60. Shipping cost included in price.
Foreign Price: $60. Add $15 per copy for shipping.
Order from **newparadigm.schillerinstitute.com**
Tel 1 703 297 8368

What Will It Take to Defeat the Russiagate Coup and Bring the U.S. and Europe into the New Paradigm?

This is the edited transcript of the Schiller Institute's October 4, 2018 New Paradigm webcast with Helga Zepp-LaRouche, founder of the Schiller Institutes. She is interviewed by Harley Schlanger. A video of the webcast is available.

Harley Schlanger: Hello, I'm Harley Schlanger from the Schiller Institute. Welcome to our weekly international, strategic webcast, featuring our President and founder, Helga Zepp-LaRouche. Earlier this week, Helga spoke of what essentially could be described as a clash between two paradigms, two different dynamics: The collapse going on in the West, and the trans-Atlantic efforts to provoke and use war as a way of maintaining some semblance of control; and on the other side, the continued emergence of the New Paradigm around the New Silk Road, the Chinese Belt and Road Initiative, and a diplomatic offensive which includes some aspects of what President Trump is trying to do, as he's under assault from the British.

British Empire Psywar

We've had some new developments, just before the webcast, that Helga was telling me about—charges from the British of new cyber-attacks by the GRU, Russian military intelligence. Why don't we start with that?

Helga Zepp-LaRouche: This is obviously part of a strategic building up of a scenario of complete hysteria, Russophobia, Sinophobia, everything to influence the environment around the U.S. midterm elections. That is really the timing and the focus. The British are now claiming that they have new evidence that there were many Russian cyber-attacks and that for the first time they say they have absolute proof that it was the GRU; and then Holland also chimed in, calling in the Russian ambassador, telling him this has to stop, claiming that already in April, Russia's GRU spied on the headquarters of the Organization for the Prohibition of Chemical Weapons (OPCW) in The Hague, and basically creating a complete hysteria.

Supreme Court Nominee Brett Kavanaugh at Sexual Assault Hearing, Sept. 27, 2018.

Now, I'm not in a position at this point to say whether this happened or not, but one thing is very clear: Given what the U.S. NSA and the British GCHQ are doing—spying on everything and everyone around the globe—these charges are really a lot of psywar, and I think we should not get confused by it. Because for many people it should be clear, that we are in a countdown. Early voting has already begun in several states in the United States and five weeks remain before the November 6 elections, and everything is geared to defeating the Republicans with such a margin in Congress that then the Democrats can line up, possibly with the neo-cons in the Republican Party, and go for an impeachment of President Trump.

This is a heated-up environment in which every tool is being used to create hysteria. I think it is very dangerous. At one of his recent Make America Great Again rallies, Trump said the Democrats have gone completely crazy, and that the only thing motivating them is to destroy and take apart every structure and just go absolutely crazy. I think he's on the mark. Because what is happening around this Kavanaugh story is really incredible: 90% of all the news media discuss nothing but that. Paul Craig Roberts asked a very useful question, saying, why are we discussing Kavanaugh, when there is a genocide going on in Yemen, which is without precedent?

So people should really not fall for all the confetti, because the issue is whether Trump can defeat this coup apparatus against him and survive into the second half of his four-year term as President, which could

happen. A big step in this direction could be when Deputy Attorney General Rosenstein testifies in Congress on Oct. 11 and the coup plotters are all exposed. And if the American public can see all the documents which are now in the process of being declassified, Trump could have the second half of his term, where he would be really free to do what he has promised all along, that is, to get a relationship with Russia on a good footing, and eventually find a solution to this unholy trade war with China, the potential for which I think still exists. Then we are in a completely New Paradigm.

So I would say, for the next five weeks, expect the psywar and orchestration of scandals to escalate, the aim of which is to get people so hyped up that Trump can be gotten out of the White House. That is what I think is the basis for all of these developments.

Trump Strikes Back vs. Sexual McCarthyism

Schlanger: It should not be surprising at all, knowing how the British work, that they would be putting up new charges, given that they're completely on the defensive after Trump's order to declassify the documents. And also, George Papadopoulos and others are pointing to the centrality of the British role in setting up Russiagate. This is the way the British operate, and the new attacks on Russia, whatever they're claiming now about the GRU, they're still running the Skripal affair, they're still warning about Russian "genocide" in Syria, and as you pointed out, they're ignoring the Saudi operations which are committing genocide in Yemen.

Besides the constant anti-Trump drumbeat from the media, President Trump is going out on the campaign trail and has large rallies in Mississippi, in Tennessee, telling people, "Vote as though I'm on the ballot!" From the indications we're getting, it looks as though he's getting a response.

Zepp-LaRouche: Yes. I think in Tennessee tens of thousands came. Requests for tickets totaled 92,000, and, as in many other rallies, there was much more overflow than the organizers could handle, so it was

President Donald Trump speaking to a rally in Southaven, Mississippi, Oct. 2, 2018.

C-SPAN

really a big, big turnout. I think that the Trump base understands very well what's going on. Remember that back in June, Rep. Maxine Waters had called on the Democrats to hunt down every member of the Trump Administration, so when they spot someone in a restaurant or gas station, they should build a crowd and push back against them. This incitement to violence has now resulted in groups attacking the offices of Congressmen *in the Congress!* I mean, this is unbelievable. There were attacks in an airport. Letters with dubious contents were sent to some cabinet members.

An unbelievable witch hunt is being created, not only against Trump, but against anybody who dares to associate with him, such as Brett Kavanaugh.

Tucker Carlson of Fox TV has made a quite useful statement. He said that he is really horrified to observe what is going on, that he grew up among liberals on the West Coast, in California, and in Washington, D.C., who used to believe in free speech, in due process, and basically liberal values; but that the same people are now absolutely against free speech, they're for undue process, they follow the principle of "guilty until proven innocent." And I think the civil rights lawyer Alan Dershowitz put a point on it, when he said that this is "sexual McCarthyism," what is going on against Kavanaugh, and practically everybody. You can basically say, "this person raped me," and did it 50 years ago, and then that person is guilty, in a completely insane environment.

This is all designed to get out the women's vote against Trump. What this does to American women is, I think, a really a very dangerous psychological process, and people should really step back and go back to the principle of innocence until proven guilty. In the Kavanaugh case, the accusation of sexual assault is not proven so far. Four witnesses testified that Kavanaugh was not at the relevant party where this is supposed to have happened. And I think Kavanaugh himself said it quite correctly, that the issue is that he was appointed by Trump, and not what he did 36 years ago.

So this is a very dangerous development, and I can only say, this coup, with all of its new facets and shapes and forms, must absolutely be defeated.

The Rogers and Wieczorek Campaigns

Schlanger: One of the leading edges of the fight against the coup, is what LaRouche PAC is doing in particular with the Kesha Rogers for Congress campaign in the Texas 9th Congressional District. Rogers is an experienced political leader; she's won Democratic

Independent Congressional Candidate Kesha Rogers Battles Anti-Trump Democrat in Texas' 9th District

OAN

Independent Kesha Rogers speaks with One America News Network's Patrick Hussion about her mission to unseat anti-Trump Democrat, Al Green, in Texas 9th CD, Oct. 4, 2018.

nominations before; but she left the Democratic Party because of the insanity we've been discussing. Today, One America News conducted a very interesting interview with Rogers, allowing her to actually discuss why she's running. Kesha Rogers' Independent campaign, along with that of Ron Wieczorek, Independent for Congress in South Dakota, are the front end of what LaRouche PAC is doing.

Helga, how can activity in these campaigns generate the kind of dynamic that will ensure we can defeat the coup? How exactly is the LaRouche PAC intervening in the midterm elections?

Zepp-LaRouche: Kesha Rogers and Ron Wieczorek are the only candidates, to my knowledge, who are running explicitly on the basis that they are in the race to defeat the coup against Trump. I think that some of the Republicans who have a much lower profile realize that that is exactly the level of the fight which is necessary. Many people are picking up on the fact. Kesha's campaign is quickly becoming a recognized cam-

Todd Epp

KELO Talk News Radio interviewed Ron Wieczorek, Independent for U.S. House from South Dakota, on Aug. 27, 2018.

paign nationwide, because her opponent, Democratic Party incumbent is Al Green, the self-announced spearhead for the impeachment campaign against Trump.

The fate of the American Republic is at stake. Kesha Rogers is a tremendously courageous woman, and I think she needs all the support. So I would urge you: Get familiar with her, watch her video statements, give money to her campaign, go to Houston as a volunteer and join her campaign; a lot needs to be done. You can also help her campaign from where you are sitting, wherever you are.

This is not just a district in Houston, Texas, but has nationwide significance, and way beyond that. When Trump won the election in 2016, my husband, Lyndon LaRouche, commented that this was not a national event in United States, but an event of international significance, and it still is.

For anybody who still needs proof of the reason why the geopolitical, neocon establishment is so absolutely freaked out about Trump, look at Trump's Sept. 25 speech to the United Nations General Assembly. He is challenging, very effectively, all the institutions of the neo-liberal system, that system which has evolved since the collapse of the Soviet Union, into this really aggressive model, which on the one side they claim they are the best and the finest and fight for democracy and human rights, but in reality, all the aggressions are coming from them. All the things which they accuse the Russians of, or the Chinese of, they are doing it!

Trump comes to the White House and says he doesn't agree with the rules of the WTO, free trade, he doesn't agree with the International Criminal Court (ICC)—a highly biased court with no real legitimacy—and he basically challenges all these institutions saying, let's remedy all this in a different system, instead. Now, I'm not defending everything Trump does. His defense of sovereignty could be more applied to everybody, which the Russians and Chinese have rightly pointed to the fact that it is not; because when the United States—and that's not Trump, it's more the apparatus of the Senate and the Congress, but nevertheless it comes from the United States—when the United States insists on extraterritorial authority in legal matters, that is the opposite of sovereignty. Now, I can see why Trump has no say in that, because of the CAATSA law (Countering America's Adversaries Through Sanctions Act), for which 98 of 100 senators voted in such a way that Trump could not veto any part of that decision, so it's a complex situation.

Trump is trying to get a different system, and he's trying to end the wars based on the pretext of human rights interventionism, and he's trying to get a decent relationship with Russia. So it's really the battle for the whole world, it's not just an American affair. Therefore, people should really think about what they should do in such a moment.

Schlanger: One additional note on Kesha Rogers' campaign: Keep your eye on her website, https://www. kesharogers.com. We're expecting some very significant endorsements coming up in the very near future, along the lines you're talking about. People seeing this not just as a Congressional District in Texas.

But by the way, Al Green's District is one of the poorest districts in the United States, and as a Congressman, he's done *nothing* to help the people of his District, while he's grandstanding as "Mr. Impeachment."

So, keep an eye on Kesha Rogers' campaign.

NATO Anti-Russia Threats with German Soldiers

Now, Helga, when you're talking about dangers in the world, as we move toward the midterm elections in the United States, the largest NATO maneuver since the end of the Cold War is about to take place. There are very wild statements from the U.S. Command, and also the U.S. Ambassador to NATO, Kay Bailey Hutchison, basically saying the United States could "take out the missiles that are in development by Russia." How do the Russians react to this?

NATO

The Italian Armed Forces will participate in Trident Juncture 2018 with 1,200 troops, making Italy one of the main contributors to the exercise.

Zepp-LaRouche: I think that they're quite aware of the fact that these are one provocation after the other. The NATO maneuver you referred to, Trident Juncture 2018, is mainly taking place beginning Oct. 25 in Norway, with Finland and Sweden participating. Altogether 40,000 soldiers from 31 countries, including 10,000 Germans! I feel particularly bad about that, because you know, the Germans should not be in the forefront of an aggressive NATO mode against Russia. Given the history, the Second World War, where Germany and Russia were in enemy positions, it is terrible that Germany is doing this. And also, the Germans should be much more thankful to Russia for agreeing to peaceful German unification 28 years ago.

I really feel bad. I don't know what's wrong with these people, but Chancellor Angela Merkel recently said that every problem in the countries of the former Soviet Union is caused by Russia. Then Germany's so-called Foreign Minister, Heiko Maas, said that Russia is increasing aggressions against Europe. All this is, if I may say so, B.S. It's not true! It's simply not true. And these people are making themselves instruments of an aggression which, if not stopped, has the potential to lead to catastrophe.

NATO

Kay Bailey Hutchison, U.S. Permanent Representative to NATO, at a press briefing on Oct. 2, 2018.

As we have discussed this already in recent past programs, the only thing that stands between all of us and World War III is Donald Trump! [See webcast of Sept. 20, 2018.] People

U.S. Navy/Michael McNabb

Commander of U.S. European Command and NATO Supreme Allied Commander Europe, Gen. Curtis Scaparrotti briefing service members in Stuttgart, Germany on Feb. 7, 2018.

may not like that, but that's a matter of fact. Should he be defeated and the war hawks get fully back into control—they are already partially in control—nothing could prevent an escalation against Russia. And this woman, Hutchison, for her to say that Russia violated the INF Treaty, which is a highly debated question and which is really not objectively true, and then say that the United States would "take out" Russian missiles! When the whole media went crazy, saying that she is basically advocating preemptive war, she denied it, saying, "I was not talking about pre-emptively striking Russia." Russian Foreign Ministry spokeswoman Maria Zakharova correctly asked: "Who authorized this lady in such a high diplomatic position to make such incredibly provocative statements? By the American People? The taxpayers should really think about whom they are financing."

So then, the U.S. European Commander and NATO Supreme Allied Commander Europe, Gen. Curtis Scaparrotti, basically said that NATO is already at war with Russia, even if it's not yet a shooting war, they're already at war—these are bellicose statements. Several years ago, George Bush Jr. was talking about bringing Ukraine and Georgia into NATO, which is a complete escalation. The discussion about Georgia is still going on; Ukraine, not, but that's only because the Hungarian government [a member of NATO], Prime Minister Viktor Orban, flat out rejected it.

But there is an aggression from the West, and there are fewer and fewer people who realize that without peace with Russia, civilization will not exist. They are the two largest nuclear powers in the world, the United States and Russia, which together have more than 90% of all nuclear missiles, 20 times or more than is needed to destroy and eliminate the whole human species!

So, anybody who is not pushing for peace with Russia is just irresponsible, criminal, and insane, and we should really not fall into this environment.

This is a very dangerous matter, and that is what's at stake with the midterm election: its war and peace, and people should be aware of that.

Pushing the U.S. on Infrastructure

Schlanger: Since the May 2017 Beijing Belt and Road Forum conference that you attended, 96% of the projects discussed there have now gotten underway. This is the target; this is what the war hawks are trying to stop. There's an absolutely incredible statement from the European Union, challenging and basically threatening to break the Chinese initiative.

But there are a lot of positive developments: One of the most important was the first meeting in Rome of the Italian government's China Task Force. What is going on with both the Belt and Road Initiative and the counter to it?

Zepp-LaRouche: After sleeping through it for years, the European Union has now come up with its own impotent counter-BRI, Europe-Asia connectivity plan, proposing to spend EU123 billion between 2021 and 2027. But given the fact that they were not able to get the matching funds for previous monies, I think we don't really need to be too concerned that this is a serious counter to the Chinese Belt and Road Initiative. China is reacting to this plan very calmly, saying they welcome it, and that the more that countries are investing in infrastructure the better. So China is not very disturbed by it. The Silk Road dynamic is simply gaining momentum.

You mentioned the Rome meeting of the Italy's China Task Force. This was a very successful event. More than 300 people participated yesterday—businessmen, politicians, government representatives, academics, media, and others. Chairing the meeting, Undersecretary for Economic Development Michele Geraci—who initiated this first-of-its-kind task force— was very emphatic, saying that Italy must not miss this chance. As he said, "A country such as Italy, a G-7

Michele Geraci, Undersecretary of the Italian Ministry of Economic Development, meets the Italian community in Shanghai, Aug. 30, 2018, during a final Q&A session to introduce the China Task Force.

they see China rising, they can only attack it in this disgusting way.

But the only thing I can say is: They will not win. Their intransigence is at the expense of their own populations for not joining with China. I'll give you one example which really excited me quite a bit: The transport ministers of the Visegrad countries—Poland, the Czech Republic, Slovakia, and Hungary—have just met and decided that they will connect their capitals through a high-speed rail system, with trains going 250-350 kph [155-217 mph]. This is really good; this is exactly what China is doing, connecting all its major cities domestically with such a high-speed train system. If the Visegrad Four, which are not exactly the most technologically advanced countries, so far, in Europe—if they can do it, well, then all the countries which go this way will be on the winning side, and those that don't will lose.

We are pushing the United States to understand that the only way it can really recover completely, is to build a fast train system connecting all its major cities, develop new infrastructure in large areas such as New Jersey, New York, Philadelphia, the Midwest, Los Angeles, San Francisco. Some of these places urgently need that kind of an infrastructure investment, because people are losing their lives commuting four hours every day, or more in some cases. Should the United States join this effort of the New Paradigm, a lot of problems can be easily fixed.

member, must not fear Chinese investments"—so very self-assured and very positive.

We talked to several people in Europe who made the point—and there is a growing awareness of it—that it is not China which is to be feared. Everything China is doing with this New Silk Road initiative brings benefits to all the countries that participate; but it is the European decadence which makes the Europeans afraid of it.

It is a fact that what China is doing today is acting on all the values which used to be typical German values: industriousness, effectiveness, reliability, punctuality—all of these used to be typical German values. The only problem is, the Germans are no longer doing it, and China, instead, has made an incredible success in a very short period of time. It is the West that does not want to give up its post-industrial fantasies, and its neo-liberal "money makes money" speculation dreams. It is the West that doesn't want to go back to science and technology, basic research and development; they don't want to change their ways. And when

The 'Singapore Model'

Schlanger: One area where that has occurred, is what you refer to positively as the "Singapore model," from the President Donald Trump/Chairman Kim Jong-un summit on June 12, where they laid out a strategy, which was largely worked out through collaboration with China, Russia, Japan, and especially the President of South Korea, President Moon Jae-in. And now, it appears that this is back on track. It has been announced that Trump may have a second summit with Kim before the end of the year. Secretary of State Pompeo is going to Pyongyang shortly to meet with Kim.

So I think it's reiterating what you were just saying, that this approach to politics, to diplomacy works, and it goes against the strategy that was applied by the neo-conservatives with Bush and Obama, of provoking North Korea to the point that we almost had a war.

Helga, I presume that the Singapore model is an example of how this New Silk Road Spirit can turn around world politics.

Zepp-LaRouche: Yes, absolutely. And the media again were absolutely talking it down, saying it was all just utopian propaganda. But it is happening. Pompeo will go to Pyongyang. Both President Moon Jae-in of South Korea and Kim Jong-un of North Korea have said that they want to have a peace treaty, and possibly, unification—at least get the process underway—before the end of the year, and this is very good. China has offered to integrate North Korea into the New Silk Road; Russia has committed to participate in bringing prosperity to North Korea in this arrangement. I think this is all very, very promising.

So this is the Singapore model—turning a conflict into the opposite, by simply bringing in economic development and using dialogue and discussion, instead of interventions under the pretext of human rights and the whole Blair/Obama model. I think the Singapore model is the model to solve any problem in the world.

And we are continuing our campaign for a New Bretton Woods system. Because, as we've discussed many times, the danger of a financial crash is absolutely with us. The reverse carry trade from the emerging markets into the dollar—because of the interest-rate increase by the Federal Reserve—is going on. We're sitting on a powder keg.

This threat is avoided *only* if we go to the New Paradigm, a new credit system in the tradition of the old Bretton Woods, but without the mistakes which were added by Churchill and Truman after Roosevelt was dead, a New Bretton Woods which gives absolutely the ability for development to every country in the world. Glass-Steagall eliminates the casino economy; go to National Banking in every country; have long-term, multilateral treaty arrangements for large projects among many countries in the world; and go for a higher economic platform by increasing productivity—do that by focussing on such high-end research and technology areas as fusion power and cooperation in space exploration. Increase the productivity of the world economy! We could form a world so beautiful to live in—what Xi Jinping and President Trump, and also President Putin, have said, repeatedly, that we could create a beautiful world.

And what is human life all about, but that we use our lives to get a better human race? And I think right now that is what is most needed. Trump was elected because the population in the United States rejected what has happened to the youth, the opiate epidemic, the suicide rates. The same was the case in the Brexit vote, the Italian vote, the Austrian vote, and now the Mexican vote. There is a sort of international tendency, where people do not want institutions associated with the neo-liberal model.

And the neo-liberal establishment just doesn't want to get it: They keep saying, we have to insist on our rules, on our control, on our status quo. But I think there is an undercurrent, which I hope will determine the outcome of the midterm elections in the United States, an undercurrent of wanting to have development and a more beautiful world, all across the world: it exists in Africa; it exists even in many European nations, eastern Europe, southern Europe, countries that want to be hubs of the New Silk Road, and be part of the New Paradigm.

Get Aboard the New Paradigm!

I think we are actually at a very exciting moment in history. So don't be passive; get on board with the Schiller Institute. Sign our petition for a New Bretton Woods. Spread the word of this webcast—and just get active with us, because, actually it's a joyful moment in history to be alive and to be active.

Schlanger: I think people should be encouraged by what you've just reported. We do want to expand the outreach of the Schiller Institute website. You can do that—you can talk to your friends, send out posts, wherever you can.

And, to come back to what we were talking about earlier: Check out the https://www.kesharogers.com website and become active in the midterm elections.

Helga, is there anything else you want to cover?

Zepp-LaRouche: Well, I actually want to make you, our audience, curious. Because some nice, very good news will happen in the next day or so around Kesha Rogers' campaign: So look forward to it, and don't miss it!

Schlanger: OK. So with that, we'll see you next week.

May 6, 1995

No Limits to Growth: Cantor's Concept of Infinity in Economic Science

by Lyndon H. LaRouche, Jr.

This speech was given as the keynote address to the Schiller Institute's seminar in Halle, Germany, on May 6, 1995. A few brief, inaudible passages in the audiotape are indicated in the transcript by ellipses or bracketed notes from the editor.

In 1854, at the conclusion of his habilitation dissertation, Bernhard Riemann, a protégé of Carl Friedrich Gauss and of Lejeune Dirichlet, made the following statement, which, together with the dissertation as a whole, represented, for those who were willing to understand, an absolute revolution in mathematics and mathematical physics. The statement is simple. Having made his remarks on mathematics, he said, "This path leads out into the domain of another science, into the realm of physics, into which the nature of this present occasion"—referring to the habilitation on mathematics—"does not permit us to enter."

This same observation was made, as I shall indicate, about 2,300 years earlier than that meeting in Göttingen (just over the hill, so to speak), by Plato. The particular work in Plato (and there are many which are relevant to this point), which is most relevant to the content of Cantor's work, is the famous "Parmenides" paradox, or the ontological paradox in "Parmenides," which is what Cantor is addressing.

Then, of course, about 30 years after that habilitation dissertation by Riemann, we had the *Grundlagen*[1] and some other writings and letters by Cantor, which also attacked the same problem, but from a completely different method. The method of Riemann was the method of geometry; and, although Cantor makes reference to geometry, his method is not that of Riemann, but rather of one of his teachers, Karl Weierstrass. So there's a difference in method between the two approaches, though they converge on the same conclusion.

Also notable is that, during the middle of the 1880s, as in the *Mitteilungen*[2] and in later writings, the statements of Cantor on the subject of Plato are *very significant* for a better understanding of both Cantor and Riemann. That is, Cantor emphasizes that the universe that exists, is the universe of the *Becoming,* not a fixed, empty space-time with objects floating around in it. And that is, he says, the *Transfinite,* by which he means, inclusively, what becomes known as the Aleph series. He identifies the *Good* of Plato as his notion of the *Absolute,* of God.

Less than 100 years after Riemann presented his habilitation dissertation, I was in the midst of a major work, probably the most important, in terms of practical results, in my life, in refuting what I knew to be the immoral and absurd doctrines of two Twentieth-century gentlemen: one, Norbert Wiener, of the so-called information theory, and what goes with it; and the other, John Von Neumann, a man whom I've described often enough as virtually an *idiot savant,* a man whose head could juggle mathematical symbols at a great rate, and great numbers, but could *never* actually master a scientific concept.

In the course of this, I developed a solution to this problem, of how to refute these two gentlemen, based on

---

1. Georg Cantor, *Grundlagen einer Allgemeinen Mannigfaltigkeitslehre*; first English translation by Uwe Parpart, "Foundations of a General Theory of Manifolds, A Mathematical-Philosophical Study in the Theory of the Infinite," *The Campaigner,* January-February 1976.

2. "Mitteilungen zur Lehre vom Transfiniten," in Ernest Zermelo (ed.), *Georg Cantor: Gesammelte Abhandlungen mathematichen und philosophischen Inhalts* (Berlin: Springer-Verlag, 1990). The title can be translated as "Communications on the Theory of the Transfinite"; there is no published English translation.

Klaus-Dieter Häge

Lyndon LaRouche speaks in Halle, Germany, where Cantor spent much of his life.

the work I'd done earlier in refuting Kant, in defense of Leibniz. But the question was: Having made this discovery, how could it be made representable? How could we apply the discovery which I had elaborated in terms of economics, to *measure,* as we must, in making economic or related policy, or in measuring certain kinds of results?

In that context, I came across Cantor's work, especially the *Beiträge,*[3] which I spent about six months struggling through, before getting some comprehension of what the work was. Then, on the basis of having read Cantor, including the *Beiträge,* particularly the important notion of the *power series,* the power set, I returned to read Riemann again, and this time with proper understanding.

Riemann's Discovery

To situate this matter, let me first indicate what Riemann's discovery is, why it is so fundamental, and why it leads to a notion of physical science which is directly contrary to that which is generally accepted still today,

in the university classroom. The conception of mathematics and physical science as defined by Riemann's successful discovery as a young professor, is *still* not understood today, and *refused absolutely* in what is generally accepted as the notion of scientific method, both in mathematics as such and in physics in general, in the university classroom of today, and is also rejected, absolutely, by the *Brotgelehrten* ["bread scholars"—ed.] who are called today's economists, who know nothing, but who have much authority to speak about it at great length.

Riemann's discovery is a simple one, which, in principle, was known before him. It was known first by Plato, in a formal, rigorous way, and then it was addressed by others, including Leibniz. But, as Riemann says, the problem of geometry had not been effectively attacked up to his time, from a formal standpoint. He had a discovery in this connection, and had spent from about March of 1853 through June of 1854 on a special research permission on the university campus at Göttingen, to do research into every possible source, to determine if there were any indications in previous writings in mathematics and physics, which might pertain to his insight about the problem of geometry. He said he found only a couple of references, and emphasized the notions of general curvature of curved surfaces by Gauss, as being the only method by which you could attack, practically, the problem of geometry as he understood it.

Let me state the problem in my own terms, because those are more relevant to what I shall treat from this standpoint later in my presentation.

In Euclidean geometry, or any similar geometry, we use two methods. One is the method of construction, the other is the method of so-called deductive or inductive proof. In that case, given a proposition, we submit the proposition to the principles of existing geometry. And we reject, as a proposition, at least as a theorem of that geometry, any proposition which is *inconsistent* with the existing body of so-called proven theorems.

Now, this implies, especially from a Socratic standpoint (and this, of course, is famously reflected in Euclid in part—not adequately, but in part), that what makes it possible to combine all theorems into a set of mutually consistent propositions, defines certain common or underlying assumptions in that geometry. These assumptions are called, classically, *axioms and postulates.* A *theorem-lattice* so defined is, in a formal sense, viewed as a collection of interdependent, that is, not inconsistent, axioms and postulates, none of which

---

3. *Beiträge zur Begründung der transfiniten Mengenlehre*; English translation by Philip E.B. Jourdain, *Contributions to the Founding of the Theory of Transfinite Numbers* (New York: Dover Publications, 1955).

must be contradicted by any proposition which is accepted as a theorem.... To think about a geometry, we think not about a collection of theorems, we think of a theorem-lattice as a whole set of all possible propositions which might be consistent or not inconsistent with the underlying set of axioms and postulates.

So, in order to understand a geometry, instead of looking at the theorems one by one, we now look at the *common principle* which is referenced, by comparing that set of axioms and postulates with the set of axioms and postulates of any different kind of geometry. So we go up two higher steps in thinking from the level of theorems and propositions, first of all, to understand all possible theorems as a whole, as a kind of transfinite collection, in terms of thinking about the set of axioms and postulates. In order to understand axioms and postulates, to criticize them, we must make axioms and postulates, as a set, an *object of thought,* a subject of thought.

Thus we must think about *all possible* theorems and postulates, a still higher step, and look down, as it were, upon any particular set of axioms and postulates as merely one element of a large series.

These ideas of *hypothesis,* or rather, of axioms and postulates, have a very specific form in Plato. In a formal theorem-lattice, any given set of axioms and postulates is what Plato calls an *hypothesis.* Thus, all Euclidean geometry constitutes, really, *one hypothesis.* The introduction of non-Euclidean geometry in various ways, or corrections in Euclidean geometry—which become obvious partly with Nicolaus of Cusa, which develop in the work of Leonardo da Vinci, which appear prominently in Leibniz and so forth, and then emerge as the non-Euclidean geometries of the Nineteenth Century— is the standpoint from which we look today, as did Riemann, at Euclidean geometry, or similar geometries.

So therefore, we have to think about a *generality of geometries,* in terms of different sets of axioms and postulates, which sets of axioms and postulates are, shall we say, genetic in quality, so that you might say that a Euclidean geometry is a marsupial mammal, and a non-Euclidean geometry is a placental mammal, a higher form of life.

Riemann's work is one of the most important developments in non-Euclidean geometry, *the* most important, because it attacked explicitly something which Gauss in part knew, but in Gauss's letters to János and Farkas Bolyai, Gauss admits that he had *political fears* which prevented him from ever, in his lifetime, presenting his own discoveries in non-Euclidean geometry—*political fears* within the bounds of official, institutionalized science itself.

Riemann was the first to openly challenge the assumptions of a formal geometry.

The Fallacy of 'Classroom Mathematics'

What's the fallacy, looking from a higher standpoint? The fallacy is the idea that I call "the geometry of the naive imagination."

What is considered a naive geometry, is a commonplace geometry of any ignorant man in the street who says that in space there are three directions: forward/ backward, up/down, and sideways, side to side; that in time there is only backwards and forwards. And thus we have the typical notion of space-time. In addition to that, this notion of space-time, in the naive imagination, is associated with infinite or unlimited extension, backward and forward. Up to 1963, we went forward, since 1964, we've gone backward, as in economy. So you can see how we go backward and forward in time.

It also was assumed that the extension of unlimited extension in space and time, is "infinitely divisible." There's a famous case of this in 1761, when a man who was a great mathematical talent but a personally immoral person, Leonhard Euler, wrote a series of papers, in his "Letters to a Princess," denouncing the *Monadology* of Leibniz. The argument he used was a very simple, crude, and immoral construction of infinite divisions. These are natural assumptions of a simple, Euclidean-style space-time.

This is the foundation of the mathematical theory, for example, of one of the most evil men of modern history, Paolo Sarpi of Venice, the man who did more to shape current history, perhaps, than any other single individual—at least, of all the bad ones—and his student, who was also a totally immoral person, but who followed totally his master's theory: Galileo Galilei. And also Thomas Hobbes, who was a student of Galileo, as well as a lover of Francis Bacon, who was also a Sarpi protégé; and then, of course, Descartes. Through the efforts of Sarpi's follower, another Venetian gentleman by the name of Antonio Conti, they took an obscure and rather eccentric, superstitious, Black Magic practitioner from Cambridge University, who happened to be an official of the London Royal Society, Isaac Newton, and they apotheosized him from the gutter of science to become the famous Newton, and used this image of Newton to destroy science throughout much of Europe up until the fall of France in 1814. After the destruction of the major resistance to superstition, the Ecole Polytechnique under Monge and Lazare Carnot, then the superstitious fellows, such as LaPlace and Cauchy, took over the Ecole Polytechnique, destroyed its curriculum, destroyed its pupils, and began to produce the forms of Black Magic which emanated from France around the world, called "political science," "sociology," "ethnology," "anthropology," and "modern psychology"—all of these pseudosciences.

This same tradition dominates the classroom. The appearance of Paolo Sarpi divided all of prominent European science into two currents. One current leads

---

As Riemann says, to make an advance in mathematics, you must step outside of mathematics, into the realm of physics. If you enlarge that, as I do, you will say, "Yes, this is true; but let's go one step further, into the physical economy, the process of reproduction of the society, which must become more suitable to the individual made in the image of God....

---

through people like Kepler, Desargues, Leibniz, and so forth, through people like Gauss and Riemann. The other current of science, the counter-current, is the current of Sarpi; his student Galileo; his student Thomas Hobbes, who's a mathematics student who developed sociology from Galilean mathematics; Newton; Euler, who, even though he's a clever mathematician, is a complete prostitute morally in science; and then we have Clausius, Helmholtz, and so forth, in the Nineteenth Century.

The last great scientist who can be said to belong to the tradition of Leonardo and so forth, is probably Max Planck. And the terrible things that were done, almost a Ku Klux Klan lynch mob attack on Max Planck, during the period of the First World War in Germany, are an example of how science was essentially destroyed.

There are many people today who are, I would say, good scientists, in the sense of being good engineers, and occasionally you'll find some eccentric person who's actually a scientist, who will challenge the assumptions of the generally accepted classroom mathematics; but there are very few of them who, trying that, survive. Usually, when the scientific community finds somebody who violates that principle, they will either teach him mathematics until he goes insane, or they will destroy him by other means. You might say that insanity among scientists is

mathematics continued by other means.

Now, what Riemann did in reference to physics, simply, was this, and the solution was obvious to me from the standpoint of economics. Let me take another train of thought on this, and bring the two together, to indicate this.

What the Renaissance Achieved

As I've said often, until the Fifteenth Century in Europe, over 95% of all mankind lived in a condition, in greater or lesser degree, comparable to that of human cattle. They lived close to the soil, usually in rural or other occupations of that sort, had very short life expectancy, high infant mortality, long, hard hours of work. They were ground down, and they died often and early; and they were treated like human cattle by the top layer of society, which was less than 5% of the total population of every society prior to the Fifteenth Century in Europe.

At the top of society, was a group of families who fancied themselves like the gods of Olympus in the pagan writings of Hesiod and others of that time, people who played with ordinary human beings, even with their lackeys, at whim: "Kill him." "Kill him," "Kill him," "Beat him," "Destroy him," "Destroy that people," "Destroy that village." The idea of *natural law* and the natural right of human beings, for these oligarchs, did not exist. They were like the gods of Olympus, as described by Aeschylos in the *Prometheus Trilogy,* at least the first part which has survived.

In the period around the Council of Florence, and with the development of modern France by Louis XI in 1461, through the 20-odd years of his reign, there came a new form of society, the modern nation-state, committed to scientific and technological and other progress, in the conditions of life of the people within it. The characteristic feature of this was education, as begun earlier by Augustinian groups, teaching groups, by the Brotherhood of the Common Life, and so forth, which reached out and picked up boys who came from, generally, poor families, including orphans, and pulled them into a secondary education of the type we would call today a *Classical humanist model of education.*

These young boys did not have textbooks, which was one of their great advantages. They couldn't be so easily brainwashed. You couldn't look in the back of the book for the answer. You couldn't ask the teacher, would that question come up on the examination? and study accordingly, or not study.

These children had the great advantage, in the process of having to copy manuscripts to get their own texts, of being required to understand what they were copying. And by having them copy from manuscripts those things which represented the greatest discoveries, original discoveries in geometry and other subjects, by known people, the child was induced, at the secondary level, to re-experience the act of an original, fundamental discovery in science or art, or statecraft, or theology.

Now, when that happens, you are actually touching, in the child, in education, that which sets man apart from and above the animals: the power of creativity which makes the individual, that potential, in the image of God. Only in the tradition of Moses, and especially of Christianity, does this notion of God exist, and does this notion of man exist. In no other form of society— even though there are inklings of it in ancient Confucian teachings, and even though the idea, from a philosophical standpoint, is developed by Plato—nowhere except in modern European civilization, did there emerge the practical application of the concept of God as a personality of creative intellect, and *man made in the image of God* by this quality, and nowhere else was this ever applied to define the natural rights of mankind, or to apply this as the *governing constitutional principle of society.* And this occurred, essentially, during the Fifteenth Century.

This idea of the modern nation-state was developed by *geniuses,* geniuses who were produced by this kind of secondary educational method.

In France, of course, the most important feature of Louis XI's reign, apart from the fact that he doubled the per-capita income of France during his reign, was the emphasis upon the assistance of the Brotherhood of the Common Life in creating teaching institutions which reached out to young, pre-adolescent orphans and boys of poor families, to turn these children into, in many cases, geniuses.

As a result of this educational process, there emerged, within the bowels of what had been feudal society, a growing number of persons capable of generating and assimilating and using new ideas, what we call generically scientific and technological progress, but not limited to that. As a result of that, the per-capita income of Europe, and then, through evangelization, of the other parts of the world, began to increase.

No Limits to Growth

By the time of the Fifteenth-century Renaissance, the human population had risen from a potential which is about that of the baboon (several million individuals globally), to about 300 million people, something like that, plus or minus. Today, we have *five and a half billion people,* approximately, on this planet. With the existing technology, fully used, we could easily sustain 25 billion, approximately. We have not yet reached the limit, by any means, of scientific progress. I predict that we can, within 100 years, increase the energy-density beyond that of fusion energy by three orders of magnitude, with matter/anti-matter-related types of controlled reactions. We could do that, if we're determined to do it.

So, there's no limit to man's improvement and growth. What is as significant as the increase in the *number* of people, is the increase in the demographic characteristics of populations.

For example, if we wish to fully educate a young person to the potentials of modern scientific and related knowledge, we have to send them to school for the first years of their life, up to the age of 22 to 25, some more, in certain professions. Maybe we could make it more efficient by a more Classical humanist approach; but nonetheless, this proposition, that we have to keep people in school until they reach the age of 22 or 25, or whatever, is a characteristic of modern technology.

Now, could you sustain a population of students in school to the age of 22 to 25, if the average life-expectancy of the human species were 40 years of age? It would be economically unfeasible. You would have children coming out of school orphans, society unable to pay for it. So therefore, the increase in longevity, the increase in the conditions of health of the population, conquering and eliminating disease through sanitation as well as medical science, are an *essential part* of a decent life, as we understand a decent life for people today.

That did not exist, prior to the Renaissance. So society increased not only in numbers of people, but also in the quality of life for people, in their cognitive qualities, their development as human beings; not only to educate them as human beings, to cultivate the quality of creativity, but, that when they go through school into society, they find professions and employment in a mode which is suitable to an individual who has been developed as one in the image of the living God. That's a new idea.

The Development of Political Economy

The characteristic feature of this, from an economic standpoint, is the rise of political economy. These changes were brought about not by private enterprise; they were brought about by the state. And the change

A Schiller Institute geometry workshop in Boston, June 1995. In the Classical humanist mode of education, students reproduce the greatest discoveries of geometry and other subjects; re-experiencing those creative discoveries fosters in the child that creative power which sets man apart from and above the beasts.

came largely in the changing of the character of monarchy to a true constitutional monarchy, which the British monarchy, for example, to this day, is not. The British constitution is the power of the royal families and all the laws pertaining to the powers of the royal family. That's the constitution.

But Louis XI had a different conception. He had the conception of a state which would foster education, a state which would build roads, a state which would build canals, a state which would foster trade, a state which would foster improvement in agriculture, a state that would foster science and technology, a state that would foster investment in key industries, a state that would mobilize credit to build infrastructure, to provide credit to new industries.

This was the characteristic of the evolution of society, in its good part, European society, until modern times, until about 1963. They killed Kennedy, they got Adenauer out of power, and they eventually got rid of de Gaulle when he was President. We've been going downhill ever since, with the counterculture.

This produced the higher productivity, the improved standard of living, the fostering of the means of infrastructure to make this possible. It produced a quality which is called *profit,* or if you use the term "macroeconomics," *macroeconomic profit.* This means, essentially, that to maintain this population at that level of existence, to maintain the infrastructure, to maintain the education, to maintain the science, to maintain the sanitation, to maintain that level of technology, requires a certain consumption not only by the population, by the households; a certain consumption by infrastructure; a certain consumption by various kinds of production; consumption by various forms of institutions of physical distribution of goods; and we even have to allow a certain amount to keep the state going, and some services which are quite marginal, which is the equivalent of an overhead expense. It's not productive, but you have to have it.

But this is the input. As we would say in simple, crude thermodynamics, this is the energy of the system at that moment, the energy of the system required to keep society from going backwards, from devolving.

Now, what we find is that, over and above the input required to maintain a modern nation-state economy, in healthy conditions of the state, there is a very significant profit. The nation produces more than it consumes of the things which it needs to consume. This is a profit.

Out of this emergence of profit and the emergence of the nation-state, came what was called *political economy.*

We know of four basic kinds of political economy which have appeared in the past 550 years, and we know of one new one which has been invented, which will not last very long, which I'll just identify.

Leibniz and the 'Cameralist' Tradition

The first notion of economy is that which is typified by Louis XI, by the amanuensis, in a sense, of Louis XI, Jean Bodin, with his *Six Books of the Commonwealth.* Contributions were made in England by certain people....

Leaders of the anti-Aristotelian faction in German mathematics and physics, left to right: Bernhard Riemann (1826-66), Georg Cantor (1845-1918), and Max Planck (1858-1947). LaRouche's work on Riemann and Cantor contributed to his breakthrough in economic science; as for Planck, he is probably "the last great scientist who can be said to belong to the tradition of Leonardo."

But then, in the course of the Sixteenth Century, there emerged an expression of this new idea of statecraft, called cameralism. From about 1671 until the time of his death, Leibniz made a revolution in cameralism, that is, introduced new qualities which had never before existed, going beyond simple cameralism, which is how to increase the profit of society, how to raise the standard of living, these arts and how you look at these, how you measure them.

Leibniz introduced the idea of *power,* that there's a question of *power* in economic progress. There are two kinds of *power* which he dealt with. One was obviously power in the sense of *energy*; and Leibniz was the first to recognize, actually to define, what became known as the Industrial Revolution: that if you burn or use some other source of heat to generate power, you can increase the productive powers of labor in any form of production, by, implicitly, a hundredfold, simply by the application of sufficient power, per capita, to make this possible.

But also, this is a case in which the power is not necessarily increasing, but in which a new technology added—as to make a knife sharper, for example—a new technology added to the structure of production, or something related to that, also increases the productive power of labor, always meaning, that from the standpoint of the society as a whole, the energy of the system exists, but, relative to that energy of the system, *the rate of free energy to energy of the system increases.*

That is, the energy of the system increases, according to Leibniz, as the society develops, as it achieves higher productivity. But if it is done properly, the ratio of the free energy to the energy of the system, also increases.

It was Leibniz's theory of economy which did the most to shape the policies of a new nation in the latter part of the Eighteenth Century: the United States as a federal republic. What became known as the American System of political economy, as in all parts of the world it was known, as with Friedrich List in Germany, was a product of the influence of Leibniz on the thinking of the Americans who made the federal Constitution. The success of the United States was always based on this principle.

The principles are: development of education, state fostering of infrastructure, the state's creation of money and control and protection of the money, the state's function to protect the farms and industries of its people, to make sure they're able to operate at a profit, not forced to dump their goods on the world market at a loss, and thus to develop the productive powers of labor, in order to create the means wherewith to attack the problems of society. And, despite every up and down, that was the policy of the United States from the time it was adopted in 1789-90, until 1963, when Kennedy was assassinated.

Since that time, the world has introduced the idea of

post-industrial society, or information theory, and it's gone down. But we'll come to that in a moment.

Oligarchical Economics: the Physiocrats

The second model was introduced by an enemy of Colbert. Colbert was a cameralist, and, for a period of time, he was a co-sponsor of the career of Leibniz. In France, there was a group of people who didn't like modern society, who hated Louis XI. These were the people who killed Henri IV, the king of France, and thus made possible the Thirty Years' War in central Europe. They were called in France the *Fronde*; I call them the lunatic *Fronde*.

They were always treasonous to France, they were always Anglophiles, from the Seventeenth Century on. In the early eighteenth century, they developed a theory called the Physiocratic theory, from which the kind of economic policy you know in governments today, including the communist governments, is generally derived. That is, communism and capitalism have the same mother, exactly the same mother, and she walks the streets at night to support the same family.

The Physiocrats argued that all of these theories deal with the so-called theory of profit: Where does the profit come from which we have in modern society, as it did not exist prior to modern society?

According to the Physiocrats, especially Quesnay, who was a Venetian … it is not the farmers, or the miners, who produce the bounty of nature. They are no more than cattle. They are like animals, like cows, from which you extract milk; sheep, from which you extract meat and wool. You are obliged to feed them, as many as you need; you kill the others. You are obliged to allow them housing, so they don't freeze to death, *if you need them.* A page from Gogol's *Dead Souls,* in short.

But they didn't produce the wealth. They are only human cattle. This is what the "neo-conservative movement" says today: "They're only cattle."

Well, to whom does the bounty of nature then belong? "Nature created it," and since France was nominally a Catholic country at that time, they would say, "God." But who gets the bounty? Who has a right to the bounty? Oh, the feudal landlord. Why? Because the feudal landlord has his estate as a gift from God. God has chosen him to become the feudal landlord, chosen his family. Therefore, the bounty of nature belongs to the feudal landlord. So in anticipating Marx, you could say, "The Physiocrats believed in a 'dictatorship of the feudal class,' and attributed all profit to the beneficence of the feudal class, in allowing peasants to work."

Isn't that nice, to become a serf or a slave, get permission from this kind gentleman to work on that estate?

In this connection, politically, [Quesnay] argued (and this was copied directly by Adam Smith), *laissez-faire. Laissez-faire* means that the state and urban society must not interfere with the pleasure of the rural landlord, must not regulate rural relationships, must not tax the rural landlord, etc. The king may come and beg for support from the feudal landlord as a gift, but the king may *not* impose, as a king, a tax on feudal wealth.

The Venetian Financier Nobility

So, along came the Eighteenth Century, and there came along in Britain a group of people who were not feudal landlords; they were Venetian financier nobility. They had moved up, like body snatchers. They're like people from outer space who come and suck the blood out of the people and take over the people, in the British Isles and the Netherlands. And they believed in financial power; the big families of Venice were known as the financier nobility, not a feudal aristocracy. In England, they assimilated the feudal aristocracy into the ranks of the financial nobility.

One of the most evil leaders of this, was a fellow called the Second Earl of Shelburne, William Fitzmaurice Petty, whose grandfather had founded the Bank of England. Petty had an agent, a lackey, by the name of Adam Smith. Adam Smith was noted for his immorality. And I'll just pause on this to make the point, because it's relevant to the question we're dealing with, with Cantor and Riemann.

In the early Eighteenth Century, the theories of Galileo and his student Hobbes, were expressed by a fellow, Bernard Mandeville, who wrote a book called *The Fable of the Bees.* The doctrine of this book is that you must not impose morality on people; and the argument he made was that people are naturally immoral, and therefore you cannot make them moral. You must accept and legalize, in effect, their immoralities, because, in the manner that Hobbes describes in his *Leviathan* and so forth, the interaction of conflicting immoralities becomes the Good. This is John Locke's notion of the Good, the "social contract" idea. And [Mandeville's] slogan was, "Private vices, public virtues": Out of the practice of vice among the people, interacting with each other, the conflict produces, asymptotically, the public good.

Agents of British intelligence, left to right: Giuseppe Mazzini (1805-72), Friedrich Engels (1820-95), and Karl Marx (1818-83). Marxian economics is one variant of oligarchical ideology, according to which the proletariat secretes profit as an epiphenomenon. Engels was even more absurd, insisting that scientific and technological progress come from "the horny thumb of labor," the opposable thumb.

Now, Adam Smith is famous for this. In his 1759 *Theory of the Moral Sentiments,* he states explicitly: People must act according to their instincts, their sense of pleasure and pain, and must not inquire whether or not those actions they take, under the influence of instinct, pleasure, and pain, work for the good, or for the bad. God is responsible for the outcome of evil. That's their argument.

That's also the argument implicit in *laissez-faire,* and in free trade.

Smith went to France, under assignment from his masters in London, France, and the parts of Switzerland where French-speaking evil dwells; from there he developed a parody, in the sense of plagiarism, of the work of, especially, Quesnay, the author of the Physiocratic doctrine. What he did, was to change one axiom in the Physiocratic dogmas. Instead of the "bounty of nature," he introduced the notion of the "bounty of trade"; and thus he created the notion of the dictatorship of the London financier nobility and its merchant class. The nobility are like the queen ants, who send the other ants out to milk the milk-cows and gather the grain. They're called merchants.

The Marxian Variant of British Economics

The next step in this, also with a very slight change, was Karl Marx. Now Karl Marx didn't know it, but he was a British agent. He didn't wish to know it. He was recruited, initially in Bonn and then in Berlin, to the British intelligence organization created by Lord Palmerston, under the leadership of Giuseppe Mazzini. This was called "Young Germany." And when Marx got into trouble, he went to London, where he was under the patronage of … [Mazzini], who was there most of the time he was there, who directly created the so-called First International, and put Marx in charge of it. And Marx remained a protégé of the British intelligence service until 1868, when they decided they'd had enough of him, and they began to dump him, in favor of Bakunin. They finally got Bakunin to eliminate Marx's influence at that point. He continued to write, but he did not have any influence in the world, until he was revived, again by the British intelligence service, through a British agent by the name of Friedrich Engels, in the 1890s, when they decided to unleash Marxism on the world, for geopolitical reasons.

Now Marx, in London, under the direction of David Urquhart—the British Foreign Ministry intelligence official who controlled Marx in London for Lord Palmerston—wrote and developed, by various stages of approximation, a so-called theory of political economy. Marx made two changes in Smith's and Ricardo's theory; otherwise it's the same.

The first change, which is a good one, is that he introduces, in place of individual interaction, social reproduction. In that sense, among those in this series, Marx is the only one among the Physiocrats, among the British economists generally, who actually accepts the idea of macroeconomics.… There's a principle of *social reproduction of the society as a whole* which is involved as the determining factor in society. That's the only good part about Marx.

What he did otherwise, was to change, from the bounty of nature and the bounty of trade, to something else. Marx says that all wealth and profit come from the labor of the proletariat. Engels is most explicit on this, later on, as well. Engels insists that scientific and technological progress come from the "horny thumb of labor," the opposable thumb. Engels was not a very good scientist, he didn't know about apes, he only knew about girls, which he chased a lot. But nonetheless, he believed that man had a uniquely opposable thumb, and he believed that the qualities of the hand, with its opposable thumb, made man capable of using tools, and that man, by random innovation, using the opposable thumb (not for hitchhiking, but for making tools), actually created technology. And you will find that Marxist theory generally, especially among the radical Marxists, especially the anarcho-syndicalists, to this day, will insist upon that form: It is labor, organically, at the point of production, that produces.

What is Profit?

So thus, in none of these three types of oligarchical theory—whether the Physiocrats, the landed aristocrats; or the Venetian nobility types, the financier class; or in the case of Marx—is there a *rational,* intelligible explanation of the source of profit. In each case, they resort to a metaphysical argument. They say, in the case of the Physiocrats, that it is the land title given to the nobility by God, which secretes the bounty of nature as an epiphenomenon. They insist, in the case of Smith, that it is free trade, which is nothing but his version of *laissez-faire,* of the production of good from evil; business must be evil, and from that comes good, which is free trade; that's their argument. And from this, is secreted as an epiphenomenon, profit. Marx says no; even though the workers are ignorant, *they* secrete profit and technology as an epiphenomenon. So nowhere is there a rational explanation of profit.

Now you have another variety, which is called "information theory." According to the cybernetic information theory version, which is called the "Third Wave" in the United States, a number of people sitting around, manipulating information, bits of information, like particles in a mechanistic gas theory, somehow "secrete" profitability for the future, as an epiphenomenon.

None of them has any explanation for profit. This is quite similar to exactly the problem that was addressed by Riemann, and, by my stating what I say so far, you begin to see how I came upon this, and [why I have] here expressed, today, my great debt to Georg Cantor.

Economics Is Key to 'Subjective Science'

The progress of man, from the most primitive conditions … involves a series of discoveries, some of which we know. Language itself is a discovery. The development of language is a discovery. The development of principles in art is a discovery. The development of mathematics is a discovery. Now, in each of these cases, if we know the history, we will attribute each discovery to the name of a person, or a group of persons, because it involves an act of creativity which occurs only within the mind of the individual. Other people can have the same idea, but they have to *re-experience* the idea, the discovery of the idea.

What we call "culture" and "education," particularly when you look at education from the standpoint of the Humboldt educational principles for secondary education—the proper education is to re-experience, in the mind of the child, in succession, the most important original discoveries in art and science of all previous history. Thus children do two things: They acquire knowledge, not just as textbook formulas that they've memorized, but they have *re-experienced the discovery* of the knowledge; and thus, this knowledge is their own. But at the same time, by re-living in the same way an infant relives the discoveries of many generations before … the child is also experiencing the *power* of that creative potential which distinguishes man from the animals, that aspect of man which is distinctly in the likeness of God, made in the image of God.

Thus you have an individual who comes out of this, not merely with information, but with *knowledge,* knowledge being not only being able to regurgitate descriptions of what people did in the past, not mere contemplations, but knowledge as a development of the *power* to stand, so to speak, on the shoulders of one's predecessors, and make a new step forward.

It is also the *power* to be able to understand and to utilize what some discoverer gives to us, so we can use it. You cannot take a bunch of people who were aborigines in training, and give them modern machine tools and modern technology. It won't work. You must develop their children. You must give their children the access to all of the best knowledge we have of our culture, and theirs before us. Then they have the power, both to *assimilate* knowledge, and to *generate* it.

Thus, if we look at this matter that Riemann attacked in geometry from that standpoint, we shift our attention away from what is generally taught today: Instead of talking about "objective science," we talk about *subjective science*; and economics is the key to subjective science.

The question is: People can imagine all kinds of things which are contrary to what is generally accepted now. Well, some of these are wrong, and some of these are right. The ability to tell the difference, we call *science*. Any original change in the behavior of the individual in society, which is made on the basis of the imagination; that's your set. Now within that, some of the changes are bad, some are good. What's the difference? The difference is called "science."

The question is whether this discovery of principle can be shown to increase the power and inclination of mankind to improve the condition of mankind, to improve mankind by the standard that man is made in the image of God, and to provide greater power to enable the society to receive each new individual in a way which is consistent with a creature made in the image of God, a society which is not based on hate, but a society which is based on the kind of love which is expressed by seeing behind the eyes of another person, an individual made in the image of God.

Thus we find that certain principles of discovery lead to good results, and certain principles of discovery lead to bad results. Thus we find that geometry is somehow *bounded,* not by imaginary fences in outer space, or strange "warps" in the space-time manifold; but space is bounded in a different way.

The Curvature of Space-time

Go back and look briefly at what Riemann was attacking, and what Riemann means by the curvature of physical space-time. He doesn't mean "warp space." "Warp space" is an idea that belongs to warped scientists, it does not belong to healthy ones.

What is the space of the imagination? First of all, the space of the imagination is not true. The universe is not simply extended in a continuous manner, as various people, including Kepler and, later, Max Planck demonstrated. Space is quantified, it's a quantum field.... It is not simply extended, nor is it extended with perfect continuity in the very large and in the very small; as Riemann argued, it is no longer necessarily continuous, it is interrupted by discontinuities and singularities.

What do we mean by "singularity"? Well, it's a true singularity in knowledge. We'll get the matter *subjectively,* rather than just objectively. A singularity in knowledge comes how, in respect to geometry? Talk about geometries which are based on different hypotheses, all understood from the standpoint of a *higher hypothesis,* a notion of geometrizing. In a formal system, if you change one of the axioms, you have a new system which cannot be reconciled or derived from the old system. Even though the theorems may pertain to the same subject matter, the two are not consistent.

The difference between the two systems, as in the case of an Aleph series of Cantor's, is an *absolute discontinuity.* There is no way, by chaos or any other way, or various kinds of these figures, of getting across that gap, no matter how small it is. It's not the size of the gap that's important; it's the existence of that gap that's important, that you could never achieve perfect continuity, which is what Leibniz argues in his *Monadology,* which Euler argues against. Euler is absurd; Riemann settles the question.

Therefore, what we're looking at in physics, is our ability to master the physical universe, in terms of a succession of axiomatic changes in the theoretical way we look at the universe and govern our practice. What we're looking for, is a principle which we can use to guide us in making judgments about new products of the creative imagination.

How are we going to know whether a line of work, a line of investigation, is going to lead to a bad result or a good result? We don't know what the good result will be, necessarily, and what the bad result; but we know it will be good or bad. Dino de Paoli has already touched upon this question of *power.*

What methods of higher hypothesis increase the power of mankind as a whole, per capita, over the universe? A measurement of man's ability to survive and improve the condition of humanity, both moral condition, imminently, and the physical condition and demographic condition?

Now, look at the absurdity of simple space-time from this vantage-point, as Riemann would. In simple space-time, you have extension, up, down, backward, forward, sideways, and then, in time, backwards and forwards. But what do you do? It's empty. How can you construct a theory of empty space? Well, you have to put something in it. So you have a sense-perception. You take the sense-perception and you say, "Well, let's put the sense-perception in a point in space and time, where

Eratosthenes' Method of Measuring the Size of the Earth

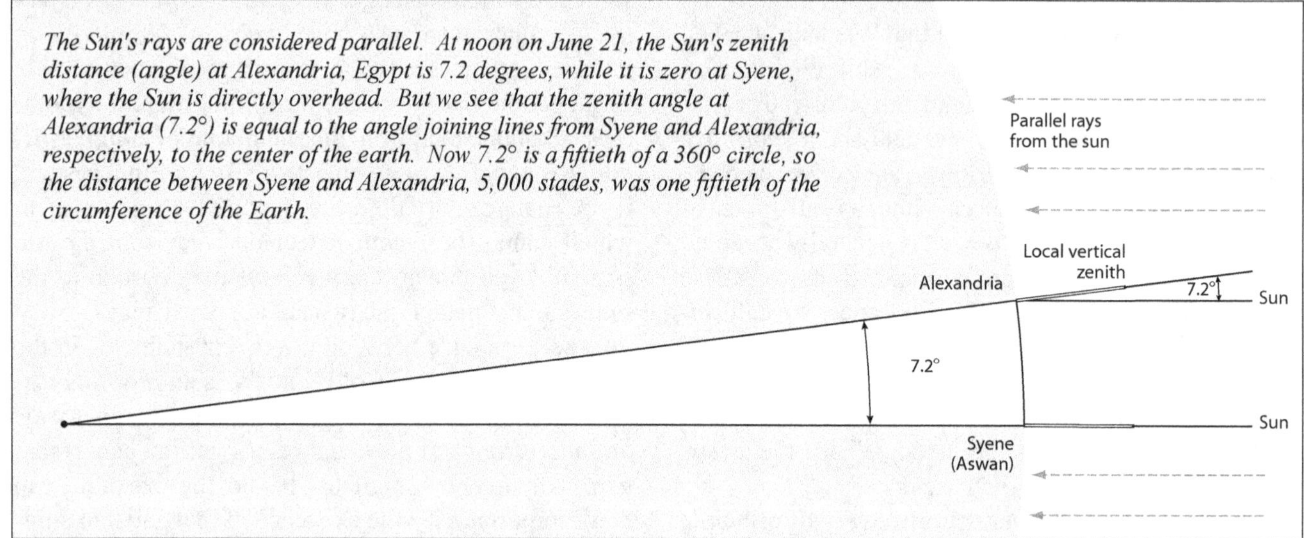

I think this thing occurred. Now, it's not infinitesimal, so it has some sides. Now I have to deal with the *displacement* of space-time by the object. Now I can make simple linear measurements among these objects in motion, and I can make calculations"—all absurd. All absurd. Because space-time is not organized that way.

So what Riemann says, is when we're looking at the relations in physical space-time, we find that we've gone through a succession of discoveries, which leads to the equivalent of a different *curvature* of space-time. It's not that we *see* a curvature of space-time.

An Example: The Curvature of the Earth

Go back in the history of mathematics, to one case that I often use pedagogically, the case of Eratosthenes, who was very important in terms of some of the work of Cantor, with his sieve construction. But it is also significant for a much simpler discovery, which is estimating the size of the meridian of the Earth [see **Figure 1**]. This is well-known in most decently ordered classrooms; but the significance of this is often overlooked, especially the significance of what I'm discussing here today.

How do you do this? We're doing it again, we're going to have it for children, because I've insisted that these kinds of things from the past, must be organized in a way that children can use them, at the earliest possible [age], as soon as the child is capable of understanding something, to have something ready for them, which is a channel for the development of their mental powers.

Construct, as we are doing. Take a hemispherical shell. Put, along the diameter of the hemisphere, inside, a stick, or a piece of metal. Now, on the other side of it, you can hang a plumb-bob, or some other device, for situating it so that it is aiming at what you think is the center of the Earth: up, down.

Now, take this at two points, A and B, along the meridian. one directly north, or more or less directly north of the other. Now, wait until noontime, which you define by the time the Sun gets into its relatively highest position. The shadow will be cast accordingly. Now, measure the angle which the shadow of the Sun projected by the stick casts upon the interior surface of that hemisphere. A comparison of the two angles, at Point A and Point B, by similar angles, will define the angle of the arc of a circle.

Now if you measure the actual distance from Point A to Point B, you have essentially approximated the measurement of the perimeter of the circle along that arc; and therefore, by simple construction, ancient people, using the method of Eudoxus, which was used by Eratosthenes, can approximate the size of the Earth.

Eratosthenes was off by 50 miles, in estimating the diameter of the Earth from pole to pole, which, considering the crudity of the methods available to him, *is not bad.*

Now, suppose someone says, "Okay, that's empirical, objective science." No, it is *not* "objective science." It is *subjective* science.

First, ask a question. Okay, the child is being asked to measure the size of the Earth. Has that child ever seen the curvature of the Earth? Did Eratosthenes or anybody who lived before him or in his time see the curvature of the Earth? Of course not. They couldn't.

So therefore, the idea of the curvature of the Earth did not exist as a sensory sense-perception. Therefore, it existed only as an *idea*! And from this idea, a notion occurred.

The same thing in Aristarchus, who said that the Earth orbited the Sun. All the other important discoveries which were made in ancient society, had that character. They involved *ideas*; they involved the use of ideas to influence the development of new ideas.

What we wish to do, is to educate children to understand these *ideas,* in the sense that Plato defines ideas, and defines the relationship between *species,* of types of actions, and ideas as such, Platonic ideas. And that is exactly what Riemann is doing. He is dealing with Platonic ideas.

This was not new to him at that point. Years earlier, before [Johann Friedrich] Herbart died, Riemann, before going to Berlin and then coming back to Göttingen, had attended some lectures at Göttingen which were given by Herbart, who was very much influenced, actually, by [Friedrich] Schiller, when he was studying at Jena earlier, and then had gone on to the No Man's Land where Kant had been to teach, and then was brought back by Wilhelm von Humboldt, for these lectures he gave. . . .

But in the posthumously published works of Riemann, these notes that he made on ideas, metaphysics, and so forth, are included. Riemann refers to these Platonic ideas as *Geistesmassen,* objects which exist only in the mind as ideas, which do not exist as sense-perceptions.

In the latter three types or four types of political economy I discussed, you would have the case of the Physiocrats, the case of Adam Smith, and then the rest of the British School, or the British School of Karl Marx, or the modern information theory; they allow only the existence of sense-perceptions, and anything else is defined as "attributed epiphenomenon," or attribute, epiphenomenal attribute, of a sense-perception. . . .

Only in this view of science [of Riemann, et al.], are ideas treated as ideas. For the formalist, ideas do not exist, only metaphysical attributions based on sense-perceptions. Every fundamental scientific discovery creates a singularity, and creates it *outside* the domain of sense-perceptions, so that man now has proven knowledge which enables him to *increase* his power over the world of sense-perception, as measured in terms of the development of the number and quality of existence and productivity, of individuals.

How Do You Measure Progress?

The question, then, is: How do you measure these things?

Scientific discoveries and related discoveries in art all have the form of metaphor; the generic form is metaphor. Every important singularity in the theory of knowledge, whether in physical science, in mathematics, or in Classical art, occurs as *metaphor.* The fallacy of information theory, is that you could never put an idea in information theory. Impossible! Because all ideas are metaphors. How could you measure the *power* of an idea according to its statistical characteristics, in terms of an inversion of Boltzmann's H-theorem? You can't do it, it's irrelevant. It has nothing to do with it.

It is not the number of bits of information that counts. Bits of information pertain to communications networks of inanimate objects, of non-living objects, and do not refer to living behavior of *creating ideas,* or communicating ideas. How do we communicate ideas? With metaphor.

What you do, when you communicate with someone, is to demonstrate the existence of a *paradox,* especially an ontological paradox. You identify the paradox by metaphor, as I've used the Goethe "Mailied" as an early form, which, despite the simplicity of the form and its almost trivial content, exemplifies this. It contains the essential thing, which is a metaphor.

Therefore, by communicating *metaphorically,* using the subjunctive and so forth with a language, we can precisely define a singularity, an irony, a metaphor; and, by communicating a metaphor, whether in the science or mathematics classroom, or in the question of tragedy or Classical poetry or music, you thus prompt the mind of the hearer to go through the process of testing the generation of metaphor.

So, how do you measure progress? How do you measure what we must measure, in an economy? What we must measure, is *progress.* You cannot measure progress in terms of some simple Aristotelian-deductive mathematics; how do you measure it? You can't measure it in deductive terms simply, because every time you have scientific progress, you introduce a *discontinuity* into your theory. So therefore, the subject of economic science is not linear algebra, applications of statistics. The subject of economic science, is the *ordering of discontinuities.*

What Cantor indicates as *power,* is exactly appropriate as the word to use, in respect to economic power. The progress of mankind, is what? The progress of mankind is the accumulation of original, fundamental discoveries in what we call science, in what we call Classical art. This is the heritage which each generation passes to the next.

What is this heritage? This heritage is a mass of discontinuities, a mass of discoveries, original, axiomatic quality of discoveries, whether in language, the use of language, or in anything else. What we pass on, is not measurable knowledge, in the ordinary sense; we pass on *discontinuities.* We call this an education, putting a child through original discoveries, re-experiencing them.

So therefore, in economics, the same thing. What defines economic progress? What defines scientific progress? The development of discontinuities. How is this measured? As the *increase in the density of discontinuities in terms of any measurable unit of action in the economy as a whole.*

So therefore, what is the significance of the Aleph series in Cantor? Its application is as an approach to the understanding of the measurement of discontinuities. Now, those who understand Cantor somewhat better, even if imperfectly, will always emphasize that, the fact that there's the implicit denumerability of a finite number of discontinuities within any arbitrarily chosen interval of action. And that's what we're doing.

Now, how do you run society on that basis? Mathematically? Not exactly. What you do, is what I've learned to do. You say, what is it that we commonly believe today, say in physical science, which is wrong? How do we define that? Let's take astronomy. You go talk to the astronomers, and find out what stellar objects or events in the astronomical domain, are anomalous, things which defy interpretation according to existing generally accepted notions of astronomy. And therefore, you say, "Well, it is important that the state consider how we're going to bring about a study of these anomalies, because we know, that by mastering these anomalies, we will correct our existing knowledge, and therefore we will increase the power of productivity of man over nature."

Take it in microphysics. It's simple, you just keep going down the scale, smaller and smaller. Every time you find an anomaly, *that's* what you must concentrate on. How do you know what the benefit is going to be? You don't have to know. Because the question of *policy,* the fundamental question of science, is not whether you can measure something in advance. Some things you can, some things you can't. The important thing to know is: What is the next step you must take? It's like walking through a swamp full of quicksand. You don't have to know how much quicksand there is, how big the stones are, how many stones there are; all you have to know is: Can you find a stone on which to walk, which will allow you, step by step, to get safely out of that swamp?

And therefore, what we need, is an understanding of this subjective aspect of science, in terms of the notion of discontinuities. A good mathematics is one which is not exaggerated in its importance. Mathematics is an engineering tool which must be constantly improved; but it's always wrong, because the next anomaly is going to overturn it.

So therefore, the important thing to do is to put mathematics in its place, as a little fellow here, who's carrying the bags for the big fellow, science. And science consists in the principles of discovery, and knowing how to make these discoveries, not in being able to pre-measure. Because you won't know how to measure them, until you make them. Then you will find out how to measure them.

So therefore, the question is, the relative power of mankind achieved by what? By … anomalies.

What is an anomaly? If there are hungry people in the world who should not be hungry, that's an anomaly. That may not involve a great, new discovery, but that means the *existing policy of practice of the relevant institutions, is wrong.* If the death rate increases, and we can attribute the death rate to some cause, like cutting of pensions, for example, or cutting the health care provisions under existing law, that's wrong, that's murder. If you cause a change in public policies or insurance policy which you should have known would have increased the sickness rate or the death rate, then you personally are responsible for every person that becomes sick or dies as a result of your innovation, contrary to Adam Smith. Evil produces evil, and evil is accountable for evil; and negligence, in that sense, is evil.

So we have to change the focus to the subject, and the important thing is that, as Riemann says, to make an advance in mathematics, you must step outside of mathematics, into the realm of physics. If you enlarge that, as I do, you will say, "Yes, this is true; but let's go one step further, into the physical economy, the process of reproduction of the society, which must become more suitable to the individual made in the image of God, both in his education, his knowledge, his responsiveness, and his accountability for the results."

Roger Stone Endorses Kesha Rogers, Independent for Congress in Texas 9th CD

by Stephanie Ezrol

Oct. 9—In what may come as a surprise, or perhaps a wave of fear, to so-called political experts, Roger Stone—a long-time advisor to many Republican candidates and a friend of Donald Trump—endorsed Kesha Rogers on October 8. She is on the November 6 ballot as an Independent candidate for the 9th Congressional District in Texas against incumbent Democrat Al Green, a fanatic for the impeachment of the President. Stone, who had encouraged Trump to run for President as early as 1988, and who played a role in shaping his 2016 Presidential campaign, has been outspoken in his opposition to the regime-change coup being run against President Trump.

He noted Rogers' record of Democratic Party primary election victories for U.S. Congress in Texas, and praised her role against what he has called the two-party "duopoly." Stone sharply stated, "these midterm elections are about more than which 'party' wins. It is a matter of whether the American people choose war or peace, a downward economic spiral, or economic development, through growing the real economy."

Rogers has denounced "Russiagate" as a coup, led by America's oldest enemy, the British Empire, against the duly elected president of the United States, Donald Trump. Stone, in his endorsement of her, all but called it by its proper name. He said "there is not a shred of evidence" of President Trump's collusion with Russia in the "Mueller 'witch hunt'," but rather there is "collusion between British intelligence networks, which represent the bankrupt City of London, and Obama's intelligence officials, such as Brennan and Clapper, and the corrupted elements of the Justice Department and FBI, who are running an unconstitutional coup to prevent President Trump from pursuing a policy of peace through negotiations, and support for the sovereignty of all nations, including the United States."

Stone excoriated Rogers' opponent Congressman Al Green for his gross hypocrisy and total lack of "concern for the people of his district, which is one of the poorest in the country," saying of Rogers, "She has demonstrated the courage to stand up against both the Bush and Obama machines in Texas, and to stand above the parties." Kesha Rogers is the central candidate endorsed by LaRouche PAC's "Campaign to Win the Future" in 2018.